A CLOSER LOOK BOOK
Published in the United States by
Franklin Watts, Inc., in 1977

Designed by David Cook and
Associates and produced
by The Archon Press Ltd,
28 Percy Street,
London W1P 9FF

The author wishes
to acknowledge the
assistance received
from Mrs. Joyce Pope
of the British Museum
(Natural History),
London, during the
preparation of this book.

First published in
Great Britain 1976 by
Hamish Hamilton
Children's Books Ltd

Printed in Great Britain
by W. S. Cowell Ltd,
Butter Market, Ipswich

Library of Congress
Catalog Card Number: 76–27970
ISBN (Library edition): 0–531–00368–X
ISBN (Trade edition): 0–531–02478–4

A closer Look at
BEARS AND PANDAS

Susannah Cook

Illustrated by
Richard Orr

Franklin Watts · New York · 1977

Bears and pandas

Brown bears
Standing on their hind legs to sniff out food—or danger—brown bears are well over six feet tall.

We all know bears and pandas from zoos and stories, and as favorite toys. But their lives in the wild are much more of a mystery. Because they can be dangerous, and because they do not live in groups or packs as many other animals do, it is hard to study their behavior and way of life.

Bears and pandas are mammals. Mammals are the most highly developed group of animals that have backbones. They have hair on their bodies, and the females have milk glands to feed their young. They are warm-blooded—their body temperature does not depend on the surrounding air. Dogs and whales and rabbits are mammals, and so are human beings.

Bears and pandas belong to the group of mammals called carnivores. This means they are flesh-eaters, but neither animal eats much meat. Bears are omnivorous, meaning they eat everything, and pandas are mostly vegetarian.

Scientists once thought that pandas belonged to the bear family, and pandas do look somewhat like bears. But most now agree that these animals are related to the raccoons.

Bears are very large, and they have very sharp claws. But even more important to them is their sense of smell, which tells them of danger in time to avoid it. They usually stay well away from people and so are not often a great threat to them. In North America, bears are sometimes attacked by wolves, and in Siberia, by tigers. But usually the only creatures they have to defend themselves against are human beings.

Until about 200 years ago bears were found all over the Northern Hemisphere. But spreading civilization took away most of the bears' natural home; and the invention of the rifle gave people a powerful weapon to use against them. Today there are large numbers of bears only in western North America and northeast Asia.

The winters in these areas are often cold and hard, and food is difficult to find. Bears have learned to live through the winters by hibernating—spending them in dens sleeping or half-sleeping.

Giant pandas live in deep bamboo forests in China, far from civilization. The Chinese government protects them with laws and does not allow many to leave the country. For these reasons they do not seem to be dying out.

Order Carnivora

| Panda
Family: *Ailuropodiae* | Bear
Ursidae | Badger
Mustelidae | Wolf
Canidae | Civet
Viverridae | Hyena
Hyaenidae | Tiger
Felidae |

Pandas and raccoons

Pandas are now thought to belong to the raccoon family of North and South America, although pandas are found only in central Asia. The small red panda looks a lot like a raccoon.

Bears

Today we know 7 species of bears. (A species is a group of animals or plants that are alike in many ways.) Once there were thought to be over 200, probably because of the many different colors within one species.

Raccoon

Red panda

Giant panda

Spectacled bear

Asian black bear

American black bear

Sloth bear

Sun bear

Brown bear

Polar bear

5

Easy to please

Bears usually have little need for their enormous strength. They are too slow to catch big, fast animals, although some species can run for short periods over 30 miles an hour. Once the grizzlies attacked the bison that roamed throughout North America, but they would have been able to catch only the weak or injured of the faster bison. As a result, in spite of being the largest land carnivores, bears have tended to become vegetarians. The vegetation they eat, in turn, has helped make them as big as they are.

Most bears live mainly on berries and other fruits, nuts, and grass. They dig for small animals and insects, and in winter will feed on carrion, the flesh of dead animals. Bears usually eat the nearest vegetation they find. The big animals need to eat a great deal, and they can't afford to waste their strength looking very far for food.

Bears have 42 teeth. They still have the cutting and tearing incisors and the large canine teeth needed by the true carnivores. But their molars have adapted—developed to be most useful—into large, flat, crushing teeth, suitable for their vegetarian diet.

Bears tend to stay in forested areas. Forests protect them from hunters, offer a good choice of food, and provide places for their winter dens.

The great bear
Bears have heavy bodies and, like humans, a plantigrade walk. This means they place the whole foot on the ground, not just the toes, as dogs do. Bears' legs are formed more like humans' limbs than dogs' legs are.

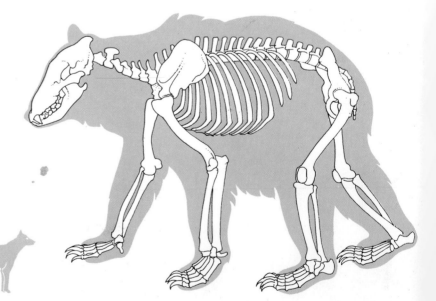

Nose, eyes, and ears

Bears' excellent sense of smell warns them of danger and leads them to food. (A polar bear, for example, can smell a dead seal from miles away.) Bears usually have poor eyesight and hearing. Their ears are small and set close to their heads and are not as efficient as the large stand-up ears of most flesh-eating animals.

All-purpose teeth

Bears have developed flat molars to help them crush and grind their vegetable food. But like other meat-eating animals, they also have small front teeth, large canine teeth for tearing, and carnassials for cutting. Their carnassials are one reason bears are called carnivores.

Claws and feet

Bears have five toes on each foot and a strong, curved claw on each toe for digging and climbing. The claws are not retractile—they cannot be drawn in as cats' claws can—but they can pick up very small objects. Tree-climbing bears have bare, rough soles, while polar bears have fur on their soles to help them grip on ice.

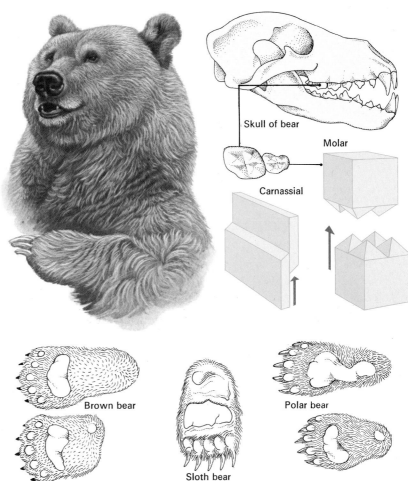

Skull of bear

Molar

Carnassial

Brown bear

Sloth bear

Polar bear

The evolution of bears

Bears evolved, or developed, over millions of years from an early creature that was like a mixture of raccoon and jackal. Later bear ancestors were doglike animals. The first true bears lived about 15 million years ago and were much smaller than they are today. Two species of giant bears lived during the Great Ice Age.

Ursus (modern bears 10 million years ago)

Hyaenarctos (20 million years ago)

Hemicyon (30 million years ago)

Miacis (30 million years ago)

Daephenodon (40 million years ago)

Grizzly bear
The Latin name for this bear describes its frightening appearance —*Ursus horribilis*. "Grizzly" refers to its gray-tipped brown fur.

Brown bears

Brown bears are found in more parts of the world than any other kind of bear. In prehistoric times—before people learned to write—North America was connected to the Eurasian continent by a land bridge across the Bering Strait. Brown bears are thought to have come to North America across the bridge. Once there were many bears in Europe and Asia, but they have disappeared from most countries. A few remain in the mountains of Scandinavia and Spain, and more live in Russia and northern Asia.

Brown bears once lived all along the western coast of the United States, but today they are found only in Colorado, Idaho, Wyoming, and Montana, and in western Canada and Alaska.

There are brown bears of many different sizes—and even colors. Those living in deep forests have rough, dark coats that help them blend in with the trees. Bears that spend a lot of time on mountain slopes and meadows, in the wind and sun, will have light, silky coats. Brown bears can be almost black or yellowish or gray.

The largest brown bears are those of the Kenai Peninsula of Alaska and nearby Kodiak Island. They may stand nine or even ten feet tall on their hind legs and weigh more than 1,500 pounds. Kodiak bears eat salmon, which is rich in protein. This is probably one reason for the great size of these bears, the largest living land carnivores.

▨	Brown bear
▨	Grizzly bear
■	Himalayan Brown bear
☐	Blue bear
▨	Syrian bear

A variety of brown bears
Brown bears can be anything from cream-colored to almost black. But most in America are dark brown.

Kodiak bear

Blue bear

Syrian bear

Himalayan brown bear

Brown bear

9

Omnivorous feeders

Bears eat great amounts of all kinds of vegetation. Black bears can climb trees and gather fruits, nuts, and pinecones to eat. But adult brown bears are too heavy to climb most trees and must eat what they can reach from the ground.

When bears meet, they will usually ignore each other. They do not make signs or signals, or growl. Usually the only way they communicate is in marking out their own territory with scratches and scent marks on trees. Both bears and pandas use these methods to show they own the ground. Bears make scratches high up on trees to frighten away smaller bears. They wander along the same paths again and again in search of food. Bears will also leave scent marks on trees as a mating signal. With their sharp sense of smell, they easily pick up such signals.

Expert fishers
The large brown bears of Alaska and British Columbia, in Canada, eat protein-rich salmon.

Bears not only eat grass, bulbs, roots, and many other kinds of plants, but actually roll up pieces of grass and roots like a carpet to eat the insects underneath. They dig holes to get at small animals and kill them with one swipe of a paw. A hillside where bears have been digging may be covered with huge holes, much bigger than needed to catch their small prey. Perhaps they dig just for fun. Bears like all sweets—especially honey. They will stuff themselves with sweet fruits like blueberries.

When winter comes, there is less vegetation. The bears find some winter berries, but will also eat carrion. They will take more risks, wandering out of the protecting woods to find food.

Rearing the young

Young brown bears
The cubs quickly learn to find food for themselves, although they stay close to their mother at first.

All bears mate in the summer. The cubs are born six to nine months later, when the mother is in her winter den. Usually the only time adult bears are seen together in pairs is during the mating season. Most kinds of male bears leave the female right after mating and take no part in raising the cubs.

There are usually two cubs and rarely more than three. They are very small and weak and naked-looking when they are born. Brown bear cubs are about the size of rabbits, and black bear cubs are even smaller.

The mother bear nurses her cubs for two or three months, never leaving the den. Bears build up a layer of fat on their bodies before winter, and the female is able to live on this while she feeds her young. A she-bear is a patient mother, but very strict. She plays with her cubs or watches them fight, but sometimes gets tired of the romping and cuffs them with her paw. She may send them up a tree out of her way. Bears are talkative with their young, grunting at them to tell them what to do.

When danger threatens, the mother bear shelters the cubs under her long fur or sends them up a tree. Then she will fight the attacker fiercely. Female bears with cubs are the most dangerous bears to meet. They will fight to the death to protect their young. They watch out carefully for male bears, who sometimes attack and eat cubs.

Whelping
Cubs are born (the whelping) between December and February. They weigh little more than a pound at birth.

Bear dens

Bears stay in their dens from October until spring, depending on the weather and food supply. The sun bear makes a tree nest. The grizzly digs a den or finds a sheltered cave. The European brown bear makes a bed of moss and twigs and lies with its paws covering its nose.

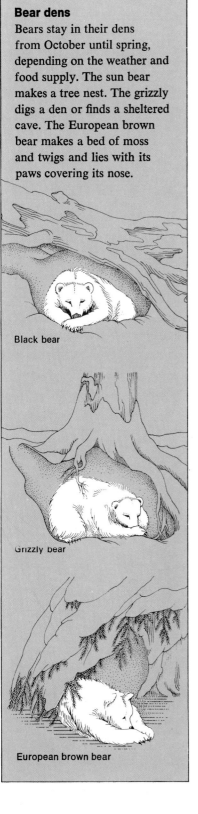

Black bear

Grizzly bear

European brown bear

Bear cubs and dam

Cubs stay with their mothers for a year or more, or until they are about 18 months old when they take up the solitary life of an adult.

Cubs and mother

Bear cubs stay with their mothers for a year or 18 months, when they take up the life of an adult bear.

Different colors
Even cubs from the same litter can be different colors, from white to blue-black. But light-colored black bears are rare, and found only in western North America. One kind is the reddish-brown "cinnamon bear."

Black bears

Most black bears have shiny black coats, but some are other colors. There are brown black bears; and Kermode's bear, which is found on the coast of British Columbia and nearby islands, is pure white except for some tan markings on its head and back. Black bears live in the forests of North America and in central Asia.

Black bears have straighter backs than brown bears, and their heads look quite different from the side. The black bear's muzzle—the nose and jaws—turns slightly upward, while the brown bear's muzzle turns downward.

Although black bears have been hunted in North America for the past 200 years, both for sport and for their handsome skins, their population has stayed quite large. They are small for bears, standing about five feet tall on their hind legs and weighing between 200 and 500 pounds. But they are very strong and alert and good tree climbers, so they are probably able to avoid their enemies better than brown bears.

Today there is much concern for the future of black bears, and many states have passed laws limiting or forbidding the killing of bears. As a result, thousands of American black bears still roam wild from far north in Canada down to the hills of Mexico. Sometimes they are a great nuisance, raiding camps, wrecking tree farms, and occasionally killing domestic animals.

American black bear

Honey hunters
Bears seem to pay no attention to the stings they receive while raiding beehives. In bear country, professional beekeepers often keep their hives high up on poles out of the bears' reach.

Funny bear

The North American black bear is thought of as playful and clownish, but it can be very dangerous. It is strong, fast, and curious, and knows that where there are human beings it will find food.

In the wild, black bears are completely omnivorous, eating everything from wasps' nests to pinecones. They will break into cabins, smashing some things and breaking others open. They have been known to pry open tin cans, drink whiskey, and even stand on a hot stove to reach food on a high shelf. They watch carefully for signs of people and try to avoid them.

Sometimes black bears kill domestic cattle, possibly because they have tasted the meat of a dead cow or sheep. But this is rare in the United States. They may also damage certain crops, especially young trees.

One non-vegetarian food these bears think of as a great treat is a termites' nest. The bear uses its claws to rip open the wood where the termites live, plunges in its paw, and licks off the insects that stick to its fur.

Tree climber
The black bear is smaller and more nimble than the brown bear. When it is grown, it keeps the curved claws that other bears have as cubs, making it a better climber.

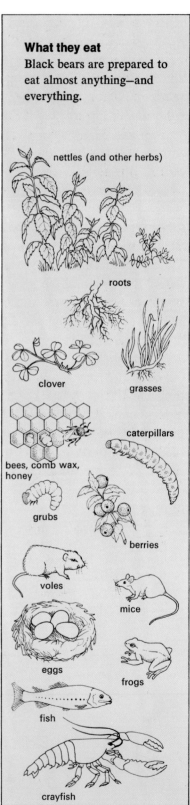

What they eat
Black bears are prepared to eat almost anything—and everything.

nettles (and other herbs)

roots

clover

grasses

bees, comb wax, honey

caterpillars

grubs

berries

voles

mice

eggs

frogs

fish

crayfish

In the north, black bears hibernate when food is very hard to find. Cubs are born only every second winter.

The Asian black bear is found from Iran eastward to Japan. It is also called the Himalayan bear and the moon bear. It has a pointed muzzle, and its upper lip is often white. It has a black coat with a white, V-shaped mark on the chest, and small black claws. Although the Asian bear stands only about five feet tall, it is quite heavy and may become enormously so when storing fat for winter. The Japanese Asian bears are much smaller than the others of the species. Asian bears are unusual in that they travel in pairs or families, sometimes with cubs from more than one litter.

The habits of the Asian black bears are very much like those of brown bears except that, like the American black bears, they are better tree climbers. They live in all different kinds of forests. In winter they stay in the foothills of the Himalaya Mountains, but in summer may climb to 12,000 feet above sea level. Asian black bears sleep for at least part of the cold season, high up in the hollows of trees. Cubs are born there in January or February, blind, toothless, and weighing about a pound at birth.

Asian black bear

Asian black bear
This bear is a partial hibernant, staying in its den only in very bad weather.

Other bears

There are some rare species of bears that we know much less about.

The Andean spectacled bear is the only bear that lives in the Southern Hemisphere. It gets its name from the white circles of fur around its eyes. Because it lives in a warmer climate, the Andean bear has a thinner coat; and, with food always available, it does not hibernate. It has longer legs than most bears and is a good climber.

The sloth bear lives in the forests of India and Sri Lanka, in rocky jungle caves or along riverbanks. It goes about at night, feeding on fruit, flowers, and insects—especially termites, which it sucks up through long, pursed lips, making a great noise. Sloth bear cubs ride on their mothers' shoulders, clinging to their long, shaggy fur with long claws and strong back legs.

The smallest and perhaps prettiest of all bears is the Malayan sun bear, which lives in Burma, Thailand, Indonesia, and Malaysia. It has a smooth coat and a yellowish patch on its chest that gives it its name. It is a very good climber. Its legs are short and bowed, and its feet turn in. It has a very long tongue, which it uses to lick up termites and suck fruit. Sun bears are often kept as pets, although they may become dangerous when grown because of their strength. Very little is known about their habits in the wild.

Spectacled bear
This forest-dweller is entirely vegetarian. In Ecuador it feeds mainly on the pambili palm, which grows almost 100 feet tall. It climbs the tree, breaks off the branches it wants, and carries them down to eat on the ground.

Sloth bear
This bear has only 40 teeth instead of the usual 42. The two upper incisors have been lost. Its teeth are smaller and weaker than those of most other bears.

18

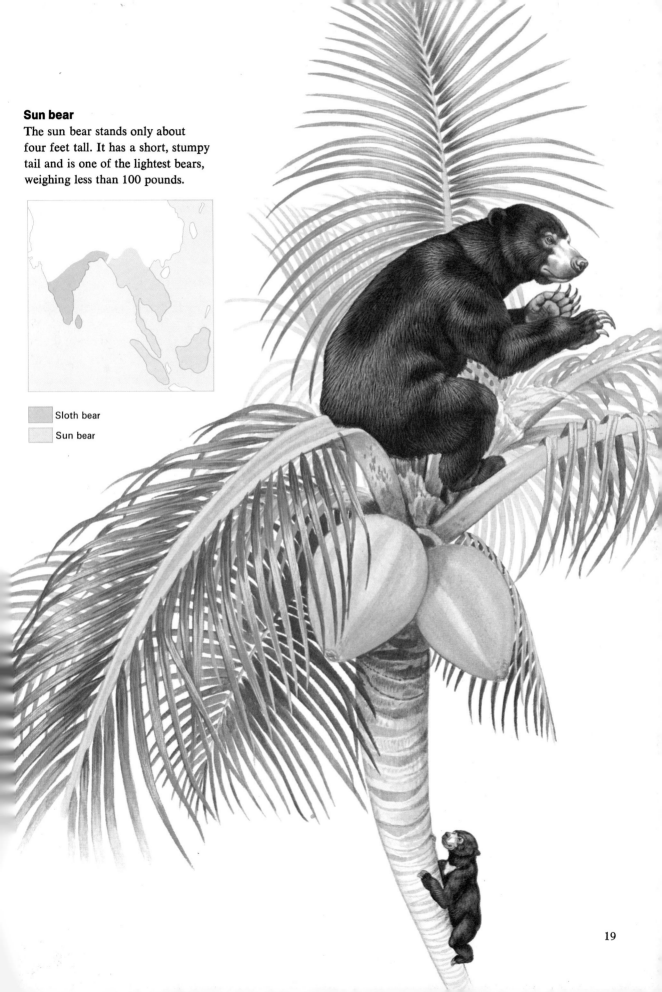

Sun bear

The sun bear stands only about four feet tall. It has a short, stumpy tail and is one of the lightest bears, weighing less than 100 pounds.

Sloth bear

Sun bear

Polar bears

Polar bears

The polar bear's home is the Arctic, and its life is very different from that of the brown and black bears. In that hard climate there is no vegetation for most of the year, and polar bears must catch animals for food.

As predatory carnivores—flesh-eating animals that prey on other animals for food—polar bears have a body shape that is different from other bears'. Their hindquarters (the back half of the body) are higher, to give them greater running speed, and they have long necks to help them in swimming. Other bears can swim too, but polar bears must, in order to travel from place to place in search of food.

Most polar bears are found on the ice along the coast or on ice floes—sheets of floating ice. This is where they find their main source of food, the ringed seal.

Polar bears are large, almost as big as the huge Kodiak brown bears. They can weigh as much as 1,600 pounds and

measure from seven to nine feet head to tail. They need their great size as protection against the cold and to help them hunt and kill.

Polar bears are white so that they can hide from their enemies—and sneak up on their prey. In summer their coats become slightly yellowish, to match the melting snow. Their thick fur protects them from the freezing cold of the Arctic. Female polar bears who are pregnant spend the winter in dens tunneled into the snow, to protect them from the cold. Some male polar bears hibernate, too, but they don't usually bother to dig dens. They find a convenient hollow to lie in and let the snow drift over them.

The polar bear's large, fur-covered paws have sharp claws for tearing its prey and gripping the ice. It is one of the fastest of all bears and, even on the ice, can run as fast as a dog.

Arctic life
In the Arctic, summer is very short, and winter lasts for most of the year. Male polar bears travel from place to place throughout the winter, sometimes great distances, looking for ringed seals.

True carnivores

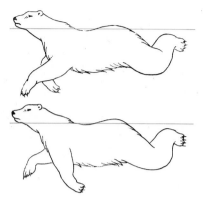

Swimming bears
Polar bears have adapted to their life in the water. Their streamlined shape makes them strong swimmers. They swim slowly, underwater except for their muzzles and eyes, sometimes for many miles.

In the Arctic summer, polar bears may occasionally go inland and feed in the icy meadows on plants like moss and lichen. They especially like blueberries and eat them until their paws and muzzles are stained blue. When they are at sea, they may eat seaweed.

Ringed seals, which are small and easily caught, are usually in good supply. When they are scarce, the bears will eat the flesh of dead whales and walrus and even other bears. In Alaska they have been seen hunting for food around human settlements.

Polar bears have better eyesight than most other bears, and a very sharp sense of smell. They are able to locate seals from very far away. They creep up on them, bodies flat on the ground. Sometimes they even push a piece of ice in front of them to hide their dark muzzles, or cover their noses with their paws. If a seal looks up, the bear will stay completely still. Polar bears' jaws are smaller than other bears', and when they catch a seal, they both bite it and batter it to death with their paws.

Polar bears have been known to hunt people in the same way and to attack small boats. They seem to think of any creature in their territory as fair prey. Their great size and speed make them very dangerous, especially in winter when food is scarce.

Polar bear diet
There are usually plenty of ringed seals to eat. But when they get the chance, polar bears, like other bears, are omnivorous.

Guillemot

Ringed Seal

Bearded Seal

Berries

Walrus

Lichen

Deadly hunters

In midwinter, when the ice is thick, seals make breathing holes. The bears make the holes bigger—just big enough for a seal's head—and lie in wait. When a seal appears, the bear pulls its head through the hole, crushing its ribs in the narrow opening.

Powerful diggers

Polar bears listen carefully for movements of seals under the ice. Then they dig through with their long, sharp claws. The mother seals are able to escape, but usually the pups are caught.

23

Lonely wanderers

Polar bears are found all over the Arctic Ocean and on the polar ice cap. They travel great distances on the ice floes that sail with the currents around the North Pole. A few have been carried as far south as Japan, but this is very rare. They are as much at home in the water as on land.

The older male polar bears start out searching for seals in early spring. The grown females and young bears follow in March or April, but they never join the grown males. The bears look for the seals' breeding grounds because the young seals are easily caught. About the middle of May the bears return to their home ice.

The mothers watch their cubs carefully and teach them to hunt. Unfortunately, one of their most deadly enemies is the male bear, who will try to attack and eat the cubs. There have been terrible fights between the grown males and females—which the females almost always win.

Mother and cubs

In March or April the mother bear leads her cubs out of the den. By now, the young bears are as big as foxes. For a few weeks they will continue to spend nights in the den.

Whelping

When winter comes, female polar bears dig big dens under the ice and snow. The entrance passages are about ten feet long. When the cubs are born, naked and rabbit-sized, the mother holds them against her stomach to keep them warm. The she-bear never leaves them, even to look for food.

24-hour-old cub

The giant panda

Red panda

This catlike animal is only about three or three and a half feet long. It lives high up in the Himalayan forests and the mountains of western China. It is completely plantigrade, with partly retractile claws. Its front paws (like the giant panda's) turn slightly in, and it walks awkwardly, with a waddle. It has thick, shiny red fur on its back, black legs, and a white face with dark stripes. The red panda spends most of its life in the trees, feeding on fruit, leaves, roots, eggs, and insects.

Pandas were almost unheard-of outside the western Chinese province of Szechwan until 1825, when the small red panda became known. Then, in 1869, a French missionary priest, Père Armand David, found the giant panda, which was at the time thought to be a new kind of bear.

Giant pandas are rarely seen in zoos. They are very hard to find, and the Chinese government allows very few to be taken out of the country. The laws protecting them have kept up the wild population, but only Chinese zoos have been able to breed them in captivity.

Pandas are much less omnivorous than bears. They live almost entirely on bamboo shoots. A sixth "finger" on each front foot, rather like the human thumb, helps them hold the pieces of bamboo. This means they can eat comfortably sitting up, rather than standing on all fours like bears.

Pandas have developed large jaw muscles and huge cheek teeth for chewing their tough food. They have to chew for about ten hours a day to live on their low-nutrition food. They eat only the tenderest piece of stem, leaving a pile of stems and leaves when they are done.

Giant pandas live only in Szechwan, in the deep thick forest of bamboo, between 6,500 and 11,500 feet above sea level. Adult pandas weigh between 200 and 300 pounds. On all fours, they measure about two feet tall at the shoulders and five feet from head to toe.

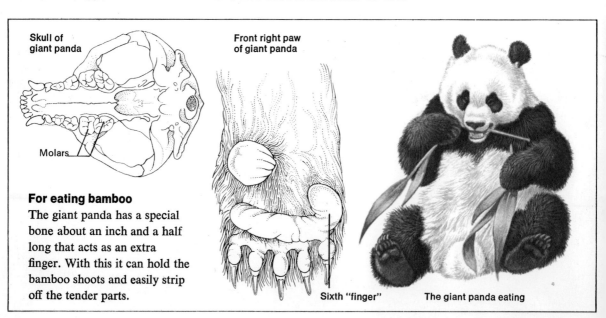

Skull of giant panda

Molars

For eating bamboo

The giant panda has a special bone about an inch and a half long that acts as an extra finger. With this it can hold the bamboo shoots and easily strip off the tender parts.

Front right paw of giant panda

Sixth "finger"

The giant panda eating

Red panda

Giant panda

People, bears, and pandas

Teddy bears
These toys were named for President Theodore ("Teddy") Roosevelt, a famous hunter, after a cartoon showed him sparing the life of a bear cub.

People have hunted bears since the Stone Age, using fire and simple traps as weapons. The flesh of one of the great animals would feed a whole tribe, and tools and clothing were made from the skin and bones.

Later, in Roman times, bears were hunted for their flesh and fur and also, for the first time, were captured alive to be used for public entertainment—cruel games in which they were attacked by people or dogs. One Roman emperor kept two brown bears chained up in his bedroom as guards.

Until early in this century, great cruelty was used in training bears. Dancing bears were led about by rings put through their noses. They were taught to obey by being made to stand on heated metal plates or by being beaten with clubs and iron bars. Their claws were clipped, and their teeth were pulled out.

In later times, people honored bears. The Indians did, as they hunted grizzly bears for fur and fat. They used their teeth and claws as decoration and their skins to make clothing and tepees. The Ainu, a primitive tribe living in Japan today, dance around the head of a bear they have killed and apologize to it.

The World Wildlife Fund, an organization working for the preservation of wildlife, has adopted the panda as its symbol.

Clownish bears
Pandas look a bit like clowns, with their dark-ringed eyes and black and white coats. They are playful when young, amusing zoo visitors with their acrobatics.

Zoo favorites

People have always enjoyed watching bears. In captivity, they are kept in national parks or zoos, in surroundings made as much as possible like their natural homes. Most zoos provide rocks for the bears to climb on, "dens," and, for polar bears, large pools.

Zoos serve both as a means of conservation and as a place to study animal behavior. Although conditions are as close as possible to natural ones, they can't be exactly right. Perhaps this is why species like the polar bear live long and well in zoos, but rarely breed. And when they do, the mother may refuse to feed the cubs. Malayan sun bears, too, are found in many zoos but rarely are bred successfully.

Pandas are usually the star attraction at zoos lucky enough to have them. However, at this time no pandas have been born in captivity outside China. Chi-Chi, the London panda, and An-An, the Moscow panda, were brought together twice, but neither meeting produced offspring. Ling-Ling and Hsing-Hsing, gifts from China, have delighted visitors to the National Zoo in Washington, D.C., since their arrival.

The future for bears and pandas

Bears, with their great appetites, need a great deal of room to live in. But more and more wilderness areas are giving way to civilization, and many animals are being left without enough room. The bears' solitary way of life leaves them with less chance of mating and breeding than animals that live in packs have. When bears do mate, their litters are usually only two cubs. These are all reasons why the world's bear population is steadily growing smaller.

Another threat is hunting. Once there were thousands of grizzlies roaming the West from Alaska to Mexico. But as the West was settled, bears were shot for food and fur and to protect the domestic animals on farms and ranches. The bears' bad eyesight and liking for open country made them easy targets, and today there are few grizzlies except in Alaska and parts of western Canada.

Bears are considered great prizes, and in some places bear hunting is very popular. Unfortunately, hunting has been modernized—in the Arctic, helicopters are used to hunt polar bears.

Where there are laws that limit hunting, bears are not dying out, and in national parks they may even be increasing in number. However, there is not always enough food in the parks for their increased numbers.

Another form of protection is the zoo, where brown bears, in particular, have been bred successfully. However, it is not a happy solution to put animals in captivity in order to save them. Zoos should be used only as a last resort in any effort to keep the bear from extinction.

Index